Cornfields, Cottonwoods, Seagulls, and Sermons

THE DREAMSEEKER POETRY SERIES

Books in the DreamSeeker Poetry Series, intended to make available fine writing by Anabaptist-related poets, are published by Cascadia Publishing House under the DreamSeeker Books imprint and often copublished with Herald Press. Cascadia oversees content of these poetry collections in collaboration with the DreamSeeker Poetry Series Editor Jeff Gundy (Jean Janzen volumes 1-4) as well as in consultation with its Editorial Council and the authors themselves.

Also worth noting are two poetry collections that would likely have been included in the series had it been in existence then:

DreamSeeker Books also continues to release occasional high-caliber collections of poems outside of the DreamSeeker Poetry Series:

Cornfields, Cottonwoods, Seagulls, and Sermons

Growing Up in Nebraska

Joseph Gascho

DreamSeeker Poetry Series, Volume 14

DreamSeeker Books
TELFORD, PENNSYLVANIA

an imprint of
Cascadia Publishing House LLC

Cascadia Publishing House orders, information, reprint permissions:
contact@CascadiaPublishingHouse.com
1-215-723-9125
126 Klingerman Road, Telford PA 18969
www.CascadiaPublishingHouse.com

Cornfields, Cottonwoods, Seagulls, and Sermons
Copyright © 2017 by Cascadia Publishing House LLC
All rights reserved
DreamSeeker Books is an imprint of Cascadia Publishing House LLC
Library of Congress Catalog Number: 2017039960
ISBN 13: 978-1-68027-009-9; ISBN 10: 1-68027-009-5
Book design by Cascadia Publishing House
Cover design by Gwen M. Stamm

Versions of poems in this collection have appeared in various outlets. For a complete listing, see Acknowledgments and Credits section, back of book.

Library of Congress Cataloguing-in-Publication Data
Gascho, Joseph, 1947- author.
Title: Cornfields, cottonwoods, seagulls, and sermons : growing up in
  Nebraska / Joseph Gascho.
Description: Telford, Pennsylvania : DreamSeeker Books, an imprint of
  Cascadia Publishing House, [2017] | Series: Dreamseeker poetry series ;
  volume 14
Identifiers: LCCN 2017039960| ISBN 9781680270099 (softcover :
acid-free
  paper) | ISBN 1680270095 (softcover : acid-free paper)
Classification: LCC PS3607.A7835 A6 2017 | DDC 811/.6--dc23
LC record available at https://lccn.loc.gov/2017039960

22 21 20 19 18   10 9 8 7 6 5 4 3 2

To Barbara,
the Virginia girl with whom the Nebraska boy
fell in love and stayed in love

TABLE OF CONTENTS

He is five now, right?

The boy sits in the second pew, beaming

A dot on a Nebraska map

He knows he will be something else

Rings of years

The only thing very noticeable about Nebraska was that it was still, all day long, Nebraska.
—*Jim Burden,* My Antonia, *by Willa Cather*

The lines are fallen unto me in pleasant places; yea, I have a goodly heritage.
—*Psalm 16:6*

Cornfields, Cottonwoods, Seagulls,
and
Sermons

Nebraska

When the boy
is asked
where he was born
he says
Nebraska
and the few
who've visited
the place
say all
they recall
is the flat flat land
and that it took all day
and then some
to drive across.
The boy wonders
how they missed
the Platte,
the clouds,
the sky,
irrigation wells,
windmills
pumping water
to the steers,
the giant combines
gobbling up the wheat.

District 37

The pump outside—
hard for little hands to move
the handle up and down
fast enough to bring the water up—
takes muscled eighth-grade boys
to do the job. The shed out back,
full of coal, hauled in by Arthur
once a month. Inside, the stove. Overshoes
on every side when it snowed. Desks
filled with spelling lists, Frito bags,
crayons (never more than eight).
The flag up front, pledged to every day.
The blackboard in the back, Aa to Zz
calligraphed across the top.

On the side, two shelves (or were
there three?) each holding thirty books:
the *Curleytops*, *Daniel Boone*,
The Life of Jesse James,
and one with cartoons showing
atria, ventricles, the valves between;
systole, diastole; electric waves
shooting up, plunging down.

He wonders where he'd be
without that book
or where he'd be if there'd been one
by Yeats or Hemingway.

He is five now,
right?

Spared

He doesn't remember hearing
the John Deere putt-putting
up the road (his dad coming back
from threshing wheat at Dibbern's)
or begging Hope to lift him over the fence
(she'd never had her own dad to run to)
or looking first left then right (must
not have) or racing to Dad on the tractor
(fast as a two-year-old can run) or the screech
of Arnold's brakes (what if he'd have hit them
a quarter-second later?)

and he doesn't recall the bumper
slamming into his leg
(what if it had hit a foot higher?)
or flying through the air
(30 feet, according to the *Cairo Record*)
or being scooped up in Dad's arms
(light as wheat straw) or his dad
leaping over the fence with him
(four feet high, he cleared it by a foot)
or tearing to St. Francis in the '49 Ford
(passed a car Dad had met on his tractor)
or the blood dripping out his mouth
onto Mom's pickle-stained apron,

but he does remember his mom and dad
speaking in low tones, time after time,
over the years, about him being spared.

Unloading the Chicken Cleanings

In her letter to Blanche, his mother writes
that her Joseph drove the John Deere that pulled the trailer
from which Alvin threw out the chicken cleanings.

Knowing Blanche, she will read the letter to her Hank,
who will look up from the *Farm Journal*
to observe that it's about time the kid starts
helping his dad—he is five now, right?
And Blanche will say *yes indeed.*

Burning the Trash

Mrs. Coleman sends him out Friday afternoons,
while the four first graders are reading Dick and Jane,
to burn the paper scraps and cleaning rags
in the barrel behind the school. Glad
to be outside alone but he worries that the wind
will quench the match before it lights the trash.

His back against the wind, he shreds
tissues, waits to strike the match
until a gust has died.

The trick's to get the fire lit.
Once set, the wind will fan the flame
into a blaze that if not watched
could set the school, the world on fire.

Lifting Weights

No gym back there with barbells,
and if there was, no farmer
would darken the door.
Weights for a boy of ten:
buckets filled with oats, and then,
when he can lug them fifty yards,
loaded up with slop.

In Sunday school when teacher Arla
turns her back, he makes a fist,
hopes his biceps bulge beneath his sleeve,
sneaks a glance to see if Donna saw.

Milking the Cow

The boy milks the Jersey twice a day.
The cat sits, waits, knows
 he'll squeeze a squirt her way.

He dreams of Warren Spahn
who they said could curve
the ball so well because of hands
made strong by milking cows when he was ten.

Before and after chores the boy
hurls the ball at the strike zone
he's made of laths on the side of the barn.
Mantle at the plate. He doffs his cap
when Mickey bows after striking out.

Schoolyard Fight

The boy learns at home and Sunday school
to turn the other cheek and that he does
until the day the bully Tommy
pokes him in the eye, smacks him
on the head when the teacher's at the board.
At recess he thrashes Tommy
to a pulp. His classmates cheer.

He doesn't tell his mom.
Once when he was four
she paddled him three times one day
for among other things kicking the cat
and breaking off a limb
when he climbed the cherry tree.
And he doesn't tell his dad
who would have taken him to the bathroom
and told the boy about his grief
and that the boy should spank him instead
before he'd have smacked the boy's butt twice,
gently with a bare hand.

The Gift

He spends October afternoons after school
gathering the corn left on the ground,
the ears the picker missed.
His father pays a buck for every bushel,
with which the boy buys Christmas gifts:
a belt for Dad, a candle in a jar for Mom.

In the early dusk, the ears
are hard to spot, covered up with husks,
half-buried, and blending with the stalks.
He learns to use his feet to feel
what he cannot see.

The Wedding of Hope and Cliff

The write-up in the *Cairo Record*
noted that the out-of-town guests
were mainly from Minnesota and Iowa
and that after the reception
(where no water was turned to wine)
the couple motored to Wyoming. No one
was surprised that Bishop Eicher
had performed the ceremony, even though
Hope wanted her step-father
to marry her. Everyone understood
that a minister was not capable
of officiating at such a sacred occasion.
What was not recorded was that
the ten-year-old boy stood
in the receiving line
between his mother
and sister, wearing the blue jeans
and tennis shoes he had changed into
five minutes after the couple, now man
and wife, had walked
together to the back of the church,
and that it was the boy
who had given away his sister
(no rules against that), and that
the boy never breathed a word of this
even to his best friend Jimmy
when he went back to school in September.

Tornados

No idle threat.
One flattened Minden,
forty miles away, drove
wheat straw into tree trunks,
twirled two-ton trucks in the air,
lifted a house off its foundation,
sucked out books from the basement
before it set it down.
Opened an oven door, whisked the plate
out from under an apple pie,
slammed the door shut.
So when the sky turned black
and the air still, the boy ran
to the basement. Dad had dug
out a room six feet below
the cellar floor, stocked it
with water, matches,
a kerosene lamp, a ladder
that could get one out
through a trapdoor at the top.

When he moves east his friends
ask him about them and he tells
about the time one hit
in the middle of the night. Mom
had been awakened by the deadly calm.
They made it down the steps
just in time, crawled out at dawn,
saw the giant cottonwood was down,

the neighbor's garage flung up
against the chicken shed, chickens
cackling away. That night he gathered eggs
as he always did. They said no way
they'd live in such a place. He smiled,
remembering the huge sky next day,
the ozone smell of air, the firewood
he'd chain-sawed from the fallen limbs
for the kitchen stove, the swinging oriole's nest
blown to the ground, fine-woven
from the colored string his mom had laid out
for the birds to use. He'd seen the fledglings
fly the day before, knew they were safe.

No Umbrellas in Nebraska

They never used umbrellas in Nebraska,
even when the rain had them running
across the gravel churchyard parking lot
Sunday mornings. The boy saw one in the
Dick and Jane book at school
and had to ask Mrs. McCullah
about the blue cloth dome on a stick
that Sally was holding up.

When he moved east
even on Monday mornings
when it was only misting
enough to switch on
the windshield wipers
for one swipe a minute
he'd see thirty umbrellas
in the hall outside the library
some prim and folded up,
others sprawled out open.

He never used one
even when he got old
and his head turned bald.
Said when the rains came
it was crazy to cover up the corn,
one needed all the help one could get
to make it grow.

Becoming a Man

Not the day in June the boy
first helps the heifer birth her calf
when Dad is in Kansas at a preacher's meeting,
or when he tears apart the broken corn auger
and replaces the stripped gear,
or when he backs the wagon full of wheat
into the narrow shed, only six inches of clearance
on the sides, just before the hail hits,

but when he turns thirteen
and pushes his niece Janet
around the block in her carriage
and an old lady with bifocals
and a blue coat stops them,
pulls aside the blanket, and tells him
what a beautiful baby he has.

The Ironing Contest

He can still remember the ironing
    contest
(only his mom could think up
something that crazy)
one summer when Aunt Nettie and
    Uncle Lloyd
came down from Alpha.
Old ironing board, sprinkling can
to douse Dad's white preaching shirts,
the heavy iron, the cord held up by a
    wire
to keep it from getting burnt.
He wonders if he had to stand
on a stool to compete.

Aunt Nettie let him win
he thinks, but ten-year-olds
can be quick
and she may have thought it best
to be slow just in case,
and to come up with some good reason
if she got beat.
He could have won
no matter, he thinks.
His mom had trained him well.
He guesses his dad had his mind on other things
when she taught him
or he just let Mom have her way
like he always did.

But then maybe he would not have
    minded.
He washed and dried the supper dishes
when Mom was sick with a migraine.

And then there was the brown shawl
the boy knitted but never wore
(no one wore shawls, let alone a boy)
and the quilt blocks he cut
and sewed together
on the old Singer—no talk
of these to the guys at school.

He lost the shawl,
still has the quilt
and remembers once
hearing his ten-year-old son
brag about it to his friends
as they rushed down to the den
to play video games.

Pressure Cooker

Mom tells how one exploded
and killed a Delores woman
twelve quarts into canning green beans
so if they see the third white ring
on the black finger that sticks
up from the stainless steel top
it is red alert. She turns down the heat,
yanks the cooker off the stove.

They all exhale.
The boy wishes all blowups
were so easy to avert.

Banana Bread

The boy and his dad drive
the red '52 Dodge pickup truck
to the Skaggs at Five Points.
They leave Mom at home
vacuuming and baking rolls
for the visitors
(who knows how many)
who will come to dinner
tomorrow after church.

Dad asks the manager
if he can use the telephone
to call home. The boy
hears him inquire
if there's anything else
to get before they head back.

But if bananas are ten cents a pound
his dad will buy a bunch without asking
and that night after chores
and after the boy has taken
his weekly bath the three of them
will eat slabs of warm buttered banana bread.

Money Lessons

He learns about money from his dad
who sells the corn just before the price drops
and buys calves, feeds them corn,
and picks the best time to auction them off,
but what he remembers about money
he learns from Uncle Edd who, every time
he and Aunt Iva drive down from Minnesota,
gives the boy a dollar the morning he leaves.
Tired of the wait (breakfast,
brushing teeth, morning prayers,
teary good byes), he finds
his uncle's wallet on the floor,
sneaks out a one and then
another one (for the offering plate
he later says). He cannot lie
when uncle asks where his cash has gone
and forgoes the Roger Maris baseball card
he'd waited six months to buy.

Blest Be the Tie That Binds

One August Thursday afternoon a car
from Oregon pulls in the lane:
Glen, the driver, two other guys,
a girl. Only three bedrooms in the house.
The boy sleeps on the couch.

Next morning after devotions,
everyone gathers around the car, holds hands,
sings "Blest Be the Tie That Binds."
Sister Hope kisses her folks and the boy good-bye
and crawls into the back.
The car heads east, makes Iowa that night,
picks up another girl,
before driving on to the college in Virginia.

Mom scrubs out the cast iron skillet
she used to fry the eggs.
Dad sits at his big oak desk,
jotting down thoughts
for his sermon in two days
before heading out to cut the hay.

Dreaming about the Appalachian Mountains
Hope had told him about, and the Shakespeare
she is going to take, the boy goes out to the field
to change the irrigation tubes
from corn rows that had been soaking
all night to parched rows thirsting
for water, wishing he'd have crawled
inside the trunk.

Plows

Only a two-bottom plow. On a good day
the boy can turn over fifteen acres.
Almost three days to get the forty
ready for the corn.

Black dirt, looks burnt.
Worms unearthed, blackbirds circling,
searching for a meal, mice fleeing terrified
from the cutting blades.

He wears no watch; he's learned to gauge
the sun, drive home, fill the tractor up with gas,
walk into the house, sit down to eat and see
the kitchen clock with both hands sticking up.

But now, if he was on the farm,
he'd have only begun; six hundred acres
more for all the corn they'll plant this year.

He thinks about the photograph
of his father in his overalls behind
Bessie and Jim, who are pulling the plow.

Irrigation

Every sixty seconds
a thousand gallons
spewed out the eight-inch pipe,
up from the aquifer
down only forty feet,
the aquifer they thought would last
a thousand years.
All day, all night,
all summer long,
the water flowed
into the ditch they dug in June,
then through syphon tubes
to flood the corn
which in fall filled a wagon
every other round.

Before the wells
his dad husked by hand—
land so ravished by the droughts
he had to throw an ear
to mark the start of every row
or he couldn't tell where he had picked.

And now the aquifer's
two hundred feet below
and sinking lower every year.

The Windmill

East of the barn,
thirty feet high,
(tall enough
to catch the constant wind),
he climbs it
when Mom is gone,
slouches at the top,
is almost lulled to sleep
by the creaking
of the vane. Is kept awake
by the steers below,
slurping water from the tank.

A hundred feet away
an irrigation well that pumps
the water to the corn, a thousand
times as much. Powered
by the lines running pole to pole
from some far-off place.

The current sometimes
stops but not the wind.

Sandhill Cranes

He lugs his big Nikon,
rents a lens too expensive
for even him to buy,
flies back to see
the hundreds of thousands
of Sandhill cranes swoop down
on the Platte, in Kearney,
only thirty miles from where he had lived.

It irks him that his teacher
never told him. Maybe she didn't know
but someone who taught
all the subjects to all the children,
kindergarten to eighth grade,
should have. Even if she did,
he thinks, she'd not have driven one mile
out of the way to see them
and would have said
that with so many birds
overhead she was bound to get
droppings (the word she would have used)
on her clean windshield.

He didn't know the walls
of her little house, half a mile
from the school, were plastered
with paintings of the cranes
bowing, leaping, dancing,
and that she had a 78-rpm
recording of a pair trumpeting,
sonorous sounds emanating from
their coiled windpipes in their sternums,
and that Miss Waters didn't want
to share this wonder with anyone.

The Wooden Gun

In the photograph taken on the day he turns eight
he's standing in front of the kitchen table,
head in a five degree Garber cock,
mouth in a Gascho grin, cradling the birthday gun—
sawed from a scrap of pine by Dad,
painted black by Mom.
No trigger, no bore, no bullets, but no matter.
The preacher's kid can now enlist
in the school-yard noon-time battles.

Dad shoots the steers they butcher with a .22
and picks off the squirrels
stealing corn from the crib with a .410 shotgun.

But the boy thought he'd never get this gun.
Maybe Mom caved in to his cajoling
and used her wiles on Dad.

At school next day, he tries to obey
what he's been taught in church,
about loving your enemies,
but ends up aiming at the head, fires,
screams, *Bam! You're dead!*

Driving Limits

His father must have forgotten he almost lost
his boy in the car wreck three years before,
because he lets him drive the tractor
when he is five, plow at eight,
and cultivate the corn when he is ten.

Still, the boy is not allowed
to drive the pickup truck the quarter mile
down the gravel road (three cars,
four tractors every hour) when he is twelve
to turn the well back on after the electricity
has blinked off, even though
it had to be done fast or the siphoning of water
to the corn rows would stop
and Dad was at the sale barn
and Mom at church at sewing circle
and there was no one else to do it.

That would be against the law.

Passing Out Tracts in Grand Island

Alone, the boy creeps up the gravel walks
to slip *The Way* into the cracks between
the doors and frames, then turns and flees.

His father knocks on every door,
and even if the woman holds
a bawling baby at her breast, he
thrusts a tract into her hand
and asks if she knows Christ.

They swing back home in time
to milk the cow, then head to church.
Afterwards they'll head
to Ralph and Sue's for cherry pie,
stay an hour, grouse about the government,
shake their heads about the dropping price of corn.

New White Pickup

Preacher farmer father, a man
who'd never had a boss, sells
the farm that spring, auctions
off everything inside the house
except what fits into the pickup truck
and moves his family East.
For the boy, new friends and books
and possibility. But for his dad,
mopping floors, plunging clogged-up drains,
clocking in at seven, out at five.

Fourteen hundred miles from home,
no coal or corn to haul,
his father sells the truck.

The boy would never know
if his father thought raising corn
trumped the stethoscope.

The Birds and the Bees

The boy held down the pigs
as his father made the cuts
that turned them into barrows,
and he'd seen the hired bull at work,
so one would think he knew
about such things.

They stop along the way with friends
first night of the big move,
and while the adults in the kitchen shake
their heads about the Roman Catholic Kennedy
running for president, the girls lead him
by the hand up the stairs, climb onto the bed,
pull down their pants, and say *you do the same.*

When they leave, the boy,
tired from tossing in his bed
alone all night, lets his mother crawl
into the front seat first,
sits by the window, nods
when his father says
what a nice visit that was.

If the Boy Had Stayed

In spring, he'd be out planting corn,
on his endless rounds,
mind working on what to tell
the flock about the difficult passage
in Matthew next Sunday.
His long-haired wife
and braided little girl would drive out
with lemonade and home-made bread and ham
that he'd bless before they'd eat.
    That evening he'd grumble
about the falling price of corn and later on
nod off, front page
of *The Grand Island Independent* draped
across his chest. In half an hour he'd be snoring,
with a smile on his face, dreaming,
about the last reunion when cousin Jim
from DC ranted about the hour-long
traffic jams on the beltway
and the Democrats in the Senate.

The Flashlight

Now at sixty-eight he double bolts
the outside door at ten,
closes all the blinds,
makes sure the bathroom light stays on,
the bedroom door an inch ajar,
has memorized the times the cop car
prowls his street
and when in bed recalls
the boy of nine who'd grab
the flashlight that he always kept
beneath his pillow,
shine the beam
on every corner of the room
and underneath the bed,
then fall asleep,
almost before the light went out.

Reminiscing about the Chores

Sipping on his Chardonnay,
watching the 6 o'clock news
while he waits for dinner,
he thinks about the cow
he milked, the dirty eggs
beneath the pecking hens,
the hay he threw down to the steers
fifty years before
and knows that at the symphony tonight
he'll see the maestro bow
when Dvorak's 9th is done and think
the man would do more good
behind a plow. But then again
neither of them would last half an hour.

Sunrises and Sunsets

He cannot decide
if the two-hour climb
to the top to see the sun
rise and the lights
from all the little towns
blinking off is better
than his memory of the sun
setting over the acres of corn,
not a tree in sight,
only two yard lights,
just turned on, a mile away.

Thoughts on Attending a January Kundalini Yoga Class

Back there Clarence would not have said it to his face
but would have told Ethel before the car
had turned out on the gravel road
that a man was nuts
to drive to some gym,
sit on purple mats
on painful folded legs,
breathe in, twist left, breathe out, twist right,
sing to the sun and light and love
before he bowed and left

when all he had to do was head out to the barn,
squat on a stool, milk his cows,
throw down bales of hay,
wrestle steers to cut their horns.

All the boy who's now a man
would gladly do, but he has no hay, no cows,
no barn to keep them in.

Jumping

No worry about him jumping from a bridge
before some cop can talk him down,
never from a plane even with two parachutes.
No urge to leap from high buildings.
But when he's ten he comes home from school
and heads out to the woods behind the house,
climbs a cottonwood, edges out
on to a sturdy branch twelve feet up,
then agonizes but finally jumps
and then climbs up and does it all again.

Why he jumped he doesn't know.

Now, he thinks about the big move
before eighth grade, the two-year stint
at the hospital where he was a human guinea pig
(given drugs no one should get,
spun around in a centrifuge,
heart cathed twice), the three years in Iowa
to try the research game.
The switch at fifty-five from sliding catheters down arteries
to reading sound waves echoed from the heart.
From plodding words to dancing lines.

He thinks he knows.

Reading the Sunday New York Times

Saturdays Dad had him throw down an extra bale
from the haymow and fill
the bucket with corn for the hogs,
set it just outside the pen,
so there'd be less work on Sunday.

He once asked Dad why Mom had him
put her letters in the mailbox
on Saturdays—won't some trucker
have to haul them on Sunday
instead of going to church?

Dad always filled up the Ford with gas
on Fridays so he wouldn't have to buy any
on the Lord's day. And if they did have
to drive somewhere on the day of rest,
Mom would pack sandwiches
and fill the thermos jug with cold iced tea
so they'd not have to pay cash for food.

He stops on the way home from rounds
for lunch and reads the *New York Times* book reviews.
He tips the waitress an extra dollar.
She's running all over the place,
the after-church crowd is so large.

*The boy sits in the
second pew, beaming*

Joseph Gascho
1841 – 1902

Mary Burkey
1851 – 1938

She outlived him by more than 30 years,
which may be why she's buried
ten rows away. What did it take for him
to move them west, from Waldo?
Cheaper land? Who knew. His kind
never stayed in one place for long.
No cemetery holds both a Gascho
father and grown son.

Was she as keen as he to make
the trip or was she, even then,
rows behind—or rows ahead?

Jacobina Roth   **Joe Gascho**
1873 – 1945   *1871 – 1954*

Alive these two were seldom
side by side—not like
their names chiseled on this stone.

He, the quiet one, who tried to keep
the peace, and she, so quick to say the words,
which if she rued, no one knew.

Left with eighteen orphaned grands,
she screamed her grief each day.
He kept his six feet deep.

Alvin Gascho
1906 – 1982　　　### Cora Irene Kauffman Garber
1908 – 2002

He never thought he'd end up
buried here, far from his flat
Nebraska land where ground
was blocked in sectioned squares.
Here in the East roads went every way
but straight. He talked of *being turned.*
It vexed him so when they were lost
on their way to some new church
where he was asked to preach.

She'd gasp, *Oh, Alvin, it's ok. We'll find
the place. It's only 9 o'clock.*
She'd also grown up in the West, but soon
found she savored not knowing what lay
just around each curve.

Grandma Garber

Orthopnea

All the boy has left is a photograph
of her with him in his bib overalls.
She is wrapped in a shawl. He is sitting
on the little stool his father made for him.
He is five. Jiggs, the dog, is looking up
at both of them. An ambulance
brought her down from Minnesota.
Her heart is giving out.

When put to bed she'd gasp for breath, beg to sit up.
Her doctor made her stay supine, said not to tax her heart.
Orthopnea was what she had. The frantic urge
to sit up straight to catch one's breath, to get more lung
above the heart, to better load the cells with oxygen.
Horrible to be held down, drowning in one's blood.

Had he known, he would have snuck
down to her room when mother was asleep,
hummed a little hymn, propped her up and rubbed her back.

Grandmother Gascho

She died two years before his time.
And now, he'd like to hear her story,
would like to hear it from her.

What did she think of the French lady
rising high above the harbor, torch
in hand, as she arrived? He'd like to hear
how glad for land she was
after six long tossing weeks
stuck down below,
pawed at by horny men,
sick in gut and soul.

Had she wanted to make the trip,
feigning tears before she left
the mother she would never see again?
Or was it hard for them to part,
the girl not yet sixteen?

Good she did not know what lay ahead.
Three daughters of her own would die
ahead of her, each leaving six behind.

The boy's mother told him how she and his father
had closed the blinds that faced the west, grandmother's house
across the draw, two hundred yards too close.

Now when he treats a man who's had a heart attack,
and when the wife speaks out before her husband can,
he gently shuts the lady up because he needs
to know the story from the man himself.

She died two years before his time.
How he'd like to hear her tale from her.

Grandpa Gascho

Grandpa lets the boy climb
on his lap (too weak
to lift him up himself) and tells him
about the trip to Arkansas by horse and wagon:
the swamps, malaria, burying a child
on the three-month trek home

and how he was caught
in the blizzard of 1888, walking home
from school, and how the family cried
when he stumbled in the door
caked with snow; they'd thought
they'd find him frozen in the field.

What the boy wants most
to remember is the lap.

Uncle Chris

Preached at on Sundays
twice a day about the heat
of hell. Slept in a single bed
all his life. Jilted?
Did another man
steal the one he loved? Was his mind
stuck on crops, the land?
Or something else? Did he yearn
to feel a yielding warmth
as he pondered wide wake
in the cold Nebraska nights?

Aunt Katie

Beulah puts on a party for her
daughter-in-law to be. After
macaroons and iced tea, the women
sit in a circle and before they watch
Fern open her gifts and after the Yoder lady
who just moved down from Minnesota
tells them about her six children in Indiana,
Beulah asks each woman
to tell the group about the most important
event that ever happened to them.

Nettie tells about the oak
crashing down on the corner of the house,
crushing the bed Evelyn had been sleeping in
not ten minutes before. Blanche talks
about the day her triplets were born.
Gertrude recalls the time she wound the kitchen towel
around Cecil's leg after the bull gored him.

But Aunt Katie says it was when
she walked down the aisle the very last night
the evangelist preached; and as she quiets,
fierce-eyed, some say *yes, of course,* and a few *Amen*
but under their breaths. No one else
can think of anything to say and so
they eat the angel food cake with white frosting
and by 9:15 Beulah has washed the dishes
and vacuumed the carpet and gone to bed.

Uncle Joe

would crawl out to the barn,
30 below in a blizzard,
to pull down bales of hay for the steers,
once broke a two-year-old mare
after she bucked him off 20 times,
limped all the way home
from the far quarter
when the wire-stretcher snapped
and cracked his leg

so the boy figures he never got
those rotting front teeth yanked out
because it might cost twenty bucks
but when Aunt Katie tells him
how Uncle Joe passes out when
they suck out a teaspoon of his blood,
and when Uncle Joe tells the boy no doctor
was ever going to lay a finger
on his prostrate, no siree,
the boy bets Uncle Joe will not let a dentist
touch those teeth even if it's free.

Aunt Ida

What hymn was that? she asks
after the boy, age five, proudly plays
"What a Friend We Have in Jesus"
for her and Dad and Mom.

After she dies, Delmar tells him
about the time she sent
niece Josephine back to Milford
because she was using too much toilet paper.

And in these fading days, the boy recalls
how Joe had come three hundred miles
from Colorado to court her, now middle aged,
worn out from rearing orphaned kin,
and that she got colitis and the doctors
had to cut out a foot of her colon
and how Joe married her sister Katie
and after the honeymoon
they moved in across the street
two houses down.

Uncle Harry

The family passes round
the penny picture cards
that Uncle Harry sends. They
gape at the beach, the dome,
the marble throne where Lincoln sits.

All they know:
the shallow Platte,
long rows of corn,
the one-room school.

In six more months
they read, reread,
his letters from Shanghai,
where he is called Hung Jui.
They marvel how he doles out
rice to hungry crowds,
escapes from bandits
when he's loaded down with cash
he's carrying to a mission
half a day away.

When he comes home,
he slops the hogs,
milks the cows,
just like before.
But they wonder why he heads
up to his bedroom as soon
as devotions are done,
why his door is closed,
why his ceiling light
stays lit long after they're in bed.

Preacher Man George R.

Shocking
that the preacher man from out east,
big enough to be a Bears'
offensive guard, voice an octave
down, roared from the pulpit,
kept the boy awake,
terrified about his soul,
promising himself,
he'd walk the sawdust aisle
Just as He Was, vile sinner
he was sure, at the big tent,
at the altar call, in case
the Lord returned,
and now the boy reads Kierkegaard
and Heidegger Sunday afternoons
after church.

Shocking
that the preacher man who said
he wished he had a son old enough
to marry the boy's beautiful sister,
ignoring the boy in overalls staring
up at him, exact same age as the preacher man's
only daughter, would fly the little boy,
in his plane, that very afternoon, for half an hour,
over Grand Island and the home place,
let him take the stick, once or twice,
dip the plane at Mom and Dad below.

Shocking

that the preacher man would
marry off his daughter to that boy,
would introduce his daughter
as the doctor's wife.

Shocking
that the preacher man never said a word
about the worldly ties the boy would wear
or any of his other transgressions small and large.

Delmar

Who would have known
that when Delmar was five,
his father dropped him off, headed
back to Colorado with no good bye, said
he could not play the parent game alone,
wife now gone, leaving him with six.
Delmar wet his pillow every night
for the next year.

The boy likes to walk over to Delmar's barn,
evenings. Delmar acts like he is listening
when the boy tells him
Don Larsen pitched a perfect game
even though he is in the middle
of milking his 24 cows and he nods his head
even though he knows
it took more than 81 pitches.

And that summer, Delmar pays the boy
an extra buck for helping cultivate
the corn and tells the boy's father
you got a good kid. He kept up with me
all day. He'll make a good farmer.
Who would have thought.

Sister Hope

He remembers when he was eight
and she was nineteen
and they drove her to school in Kansas
and he got to lug her suitcase
up to her dorm room
and he yelled "Man on the floor"
and he remembers when he was thirteen,
playing chess with Jimmy,
down a rook and three pawns,
how she knocked over the board
when no one was looking
and he remembers bragging to his friends
about how she'd won
the Hall County spelling contest
two years in a row.
But most of all he remembers
the yellow-billed cuckoo
she showed him through the binoculars
one weekend, nesting in the tree
next to the one-room school
they both attended. She said it migrated
to Brazil for the winter,
that it didn't stay in these parts forever.

Brother-in-Law Cliff

Cliff comes with his wife, the boy's sister Hope,
forty miles from Hastings, Saturdays.
He and the boy muck the barn,
spread the manure on the fields.
He takes the boy pheasant hunting,
something the boy's father never did,
helps him build a tree house.

That final spring Cliff asks the boy
to drive with him
six hours south to get the axle
for the trailer he will build
to move his family west,
says he needs someone to mind the map,
keep him awake.
The boy basks in the VW bug,
steel cocoon hurtling down the road,
talking, saying nothing,
didn't matter,
chili at a Kansas City truck stop.

In another year they live
a continent apart, the boy now
in a place with shelves and shelves of books,
a school with many rooms,
within two years a girl.

But the boy does not forget.

Alvin

They voted for a preacher
one Sunday, elected,
the humble farmer

who had been pulled
from school after grade eight
to plow his sick father's land.

No salary. Still
had to sow his corn,
reap his wheat.

The boy sits in the second pew,
beaming at his preacher dad
thundering on about

how God hath chosen
the foolish things of the world
to confound the wise.

His Father's Spade

His father would spit on it
then wipe it clean
on his overalls.

When the irrigation ditch broke
he'd scoop up dirt,
fling it in the rent.

And on Sunday mornings
behind the pulpit
he'd lay out the Word
in two-pound blocks,
each with clean, sharp edges.

Watching Father Shave

The boy, standing on his little stool,
watches his father turn the faucet tap, wait
for the water to turn hot, wet his face, brush
on the shaving cream, then slide
the razor up and down, back and forth,
like the rounds he'll make today on the east eighty,
plowing the ground. When father's done
the boy reaches up, runs his hand
across his father's chin, now smooth
as a just-mowed alfalfa field. He knows
because he's been on this perch
day after day that the stubble will return,
but he's too young to think about a time it won't.

August Afternoon

Summers after lunch
his father disappears
down the steps
into the cool damp basement,
piles his overalls
and long-sleeved shirt
into a tidy heap,
crawls into bed,
pulls up the sheet,
and falls asleep for half an hour
before he heads back to his plow.

The boy creeps in, lies
next to him, matches
breath with breath.

Now all he recalls:
the sweet smell
of his father's sweat.

Dad's Old Vest

Mornings, after he showers and shaves,
if his glasses are smudged
he tugs open the second bureau drawer from the top
and pulls out a vest.

His father always wore one
under his long-sleeved blue shirt,
even on steamy August Nebraska days
when he threshed wheat
and had to rush to keep
the farmer who paid him happy.

He sprays his glasses,
wipes them dry. The vest
doesn't scratch the lenses,
leaves no steaks that might distract.

He wishes his father could sit
with him today as he reads his sonograms,
imagines his father telling him
how proud he is that his son
is smart enough to figure out
all these shadows, but knows
instead his dad would say
*my how fearfully and wonderfully
we are made.*

Doctor Dad

His mother always told the boy his dad
had hoped to be a doctor, but had to quit
school after eight grades to plow the land.

But even if his dad had made it
to medical school, he surely would have
walked out that first Tuesday
the anatomy professor flashed
the *Playboy* breasts on the screen

and he would have learned the names
of the twelve cranial nerves his own way
because the mnemonic the other students used
contained the vagina word twice, once
for the vagus and once for the vestibular

and he would have raced down the steps
and out the door never to come back
when he woke at 4 a.m. in the call room
to find the night-shift nurse naked in his bed.

Still the boy cannot forget how gently
his father smeared salve
on the cat's sore paw, and how
the cat purred as the gauze
was wrapped round and round.

If His Dad Had Played Poker

no one would have had to tell him
a flush was worth more than a straight
(he could spout off the serial number
of his '28 Model T)

and he would have been the first to ante up
at the start of every hand
(the man who put the top tenth
in the offering plate)

and fellow players would have never known
if he held four of a kind or just a jack-high hand
(his smile the same if the corn came in a bumper crop
or if the August hail had flattened all the wheat)

but what the boy would like to know:
would he ever have raised the bet
when all he had held was a pair of twos
and ten chips left. He wonders

if that was how his father felt
that June they headed out,
farm sold, goodbyes said.

Asking Directions of Father

Until his father moved the family East,
when he was 54, all he knew were roads
that ran north and south, east and west.
Four miles south, three miles west
got them to the church; two miles west,
three and a half north to the Cairo bank.
But in Virginia he'd shake his head
when he was told that to get to Heatwole's Hatchery
to buy fresh eggs you headed west on 33
and just past Hinton, after the road curved left
and after you topped a little rise, you turned right
and went a few minutes until you got to a big oak
and then turned into a lane on the left.

And so the boy learned if he needed directions
he'd ask someone else, although
he came to realize the old man
always knew true north.

Plowing and Disking
(To his father)

His father's two-gang plow digs a deep
straight-edged furrow, a certain guide
for tractor tire next round.
Set in the tractor wheel,
drop down the plow—
he could not go astray

The disk the boy pulls half hour behind
marks an inch-deep line, a guide,
to show him where to steer next round.
If the sun is in his eyes
he may not see the mark.
He will leave some ground undisked,
some ground disked twice.

His father spends his life
setting the wheel,
dropping down the plow,
making rows as straight as steel rods.
The boy, squinting in the sun,
swerving left and right,
can only hope the ground, when he is done,
will be prepared to grow
whatever seed
will be planted next.

The Briefcase

The boy graduates from medical school
and his father wants to buy him a briefcase,
any one he wants, no matter the cost.

They find one constructed of calfskin
with gold hinges and a lock,
and another one made of faux leather
with brass accessories
which the boy says
is less likely to be stolen
and will hold his papers
just as well, thank you.

The father pays with cash,
drives home and takes a nap
before he leaves to clean
the doctors' office suite
like he does every night.

Dad and van Gogh

Van Gogh, who, before he found his brush,
flunked his seminary Greek
and fled the pulpit for his leaden words,
would have burned his "Starry Night"
could he have been like Dad
who never got beyond grade 8
and never thought Hebrew
would do him any good
but still led his little flock to water
twice a week.

Van Gogh would have given away his easel
and painted barns instead of purple irises
if he could have prayed at the bedside
of dying men, like Dad did.

And van Gogh would have said
that the shock of wheat, etched on the corner
of Dad's tombstone by some untrained
journeyman, was finer than
his "Wheat Field Behind Saint-Paul Hospital."

Van Gogh in Nebraska

If Van Gogh had lived with them in Nebraska
(the boy's mother would have fixed him up in the back bedroom,
washed his filthy clothes every Monday,
even cleaned his brushes with turpentine)
he'd have discovered, on one of his morning walks,
the sunflowers on the fence line
between their place and Harold Schweitzer's.
But if he had waited too long to paint them
all he would have found was corn. As for the sunflowers,
weeds is what the boy's father would have called them,
before he chopped them down.

To His Mother

She spanked him when he tore
his new suit pants from Sears and Roebuck
at Hope's wedding,
and some days she'd pout,
never say a word,
(Dad would beg her *why*,
she'd never say)
but she read at night to him,
about the missionary doctor
in Africa and she sometimes let him
line the people up and press
the button on her Kodak
when he was only five and
she showed him one day,
when he came home from school crying
about the assignment of writing
a story about what he had done
the last summer, the clippings
of what she wrote for the *Jackson County Pilot*,
the who's-been-where news,
and one evening when he trudged
in from doing chores she told him
what a dependable boy he was
and that he would go a long way.

Mother from Minnesota

When his wife springs the surprise dinner
when he turns sixty, and when the guests
ask for a speech, he throws out jokes
about his body parts that creak
but wishes he could thank the one

who decided, after her first husband died
six months after their wedding vows,
that she would marry the bachelor farmer preacher,
who she had dated by mail for a year, (saw him
only twice before the big day),

leave her parents and her native soil,
move with her man to Nebraska,
take the chance at thirty-eight,
of bearing a child, push and prod
to move the boy to a place
where people talked of things other
than the price of corn.

Crash Diet

When his patients come
for their yearly visit
he checks the number on the scales
and wonders if their spouses
went through the hell and hunger pangs
he and his father did
when the boy was ten
and his mother suddenly realized
after baking the Saturday sticky buns
and the chocolate-and-oatmeal cookies
(they ate them when they worked on jigsaw puzzles,
a cookie for every missing edge piece that was found)
and after homemade ice cream
every Sunday night after church
that in two weeks she was scheduled
to see the doctor and she had vowed
six months before her weight would drop
at least ten pounds but it had not.

The Skeleton Key

Dad drives to the Cairo Bank to deposit
the corn check, and Bob Larson at the bank
tells him that a Charles Starkweather
has killed five people in Lincoln
and that he was spotted driving west on US 30.

That night the boy begs to sleep with the folks.
As he walks to their room with his pillow
he sees Dad lock up the house with the skeleton key.
He watches him turn the knob and pull, once, twice.
The door does not budge.

Mom pulls the blinds and keeps
the lights on all night. The boy lies down
on the rug on the floor, not in the bed
with Mom and Dad, as he had planned,
falls asleep in no time at all.

"Soaked in Love and Prayer"
(Evelyn Underhill)

The boy remembers Mother
in her modest nightgown, Father
in his long-sleeved pajamas,
kneeling side by side at the double bed,
hands folded, elbows pressed down, praying out loud.
Through closed doors he hears his name.
Joseph.

In that parched Midwestern place
in that bedroom on their knees
they drench him every night.

A dot on
a Nebraska map

Cairo

Some engineer, back when locomotives
sucked up water every fifteen miles,
had named the town when he walked the land
and thought about the picture books
of Egyptian obelisks that he'd seen when he was five.

Although the streets are Nile and Alexandria,
the boy never thinks of Cleopatra
when he plays baseball with the Vickstrom boys
on the vacant lot next to Aunt Ida's
or when he drives with his father
in fall to dump the loads of corn
into Turner's sky-high storage bins. But
he does wonder if his namesake Joseph
would have thought there was enough grain
in the sixty-foot high elevators
to last for seven years
if the wells went dry.

Grand Island

A dot on a Nebraska map
compared to Omaha,
and on, not in, the Platte,
but to the boy at eight,
Grand Island.

Fifteen miles from home,
last five paved,
they go there twice a month
to Skags where they buy
flour and baking soda
and where they trade the eggplant
they raise one summer,
for the peaches shipped in from California
(his mother cans forty quarts).

They always visit the library on Second Street
to check out books, no more than ten.
On the ride back home,
the boy sits in the back seat alone,
fields of beans and corn flashing by,
reading *Oliver Twist* and trying
to imagine the pea soup fog of London.

Wood River

Twice as big as Cairo, twice
as far away, ten miles.
Too far to go for meat and cheese,
too small for clothes and shoes.
The village to which the letters come,
from which they go. End and beginning
of Albert's rural route.

His mother opens every letter,
reads and laughs and cries,
shares bits of this and that with the boy,
his dad, and then, that night, writes back.

Next day on his way to school
the boy takes the mail to the box,
dreams as he walks the half-mile to school,
lunch pail in hand, of Iowa, Virginia, Africa.

Rural Route 3

In good weather, mom sends him out mid morning to wait for
    Albert
who comes driving from the west, sitting on the far right side
of his front seat, left arm reaching over to steer. He lowers
the red flag on the box, pulls out the letters to be sent,
each with a three-cent Statue of Liberty stamp, and hands over
the pile of mail from the back seat. The boy runs back to the
    house
where his mom asks *Is there anything personal?*

When they move to Virginia, everything they take must fit
inside the pickup truck; they sell off the piano
to Raymond and Naomi, and Mom weeps when the couple
from Alda hauls off her parents' dining room table.
For all of that, the mailbox, big enough to hold a new-born pig,
must come along, even though out East Dad will walk three
    blocks
to the post office every evening before he leaves
for his night watchman job at the local college to check
for the monthly circle letter from Ida and Katie and Harry.

Land Too Level

One Christmas his dad makes the boy a sled—
three-quarter inch plywood, painted red,
bolted to steel tubes welded together
at Baash's Machine Shop.

With no hills to climb up or coast down,
father ropes it to the back of the tractor
and pulls the boy around the farmyard in second gear.

Jeff, one year ahead of the boy
when he went to med school,
crashed headfirst into a tree
flying down the half-mile hill behind
the hospital. Ended up a quad.

No danger of such things back there.

Who Hit Your Car?

He drives back one spring,
like Jim Burden, but doctor
not lawyer, from Virginia
not New York, not to see his
Antonia but to tend to the farm
his father had left, spirits rising
as the road turns straight, the horizon flat,
the sky vast. Farmhouses three
to the mile. He stays with cousin Delmar
and that last night, the children come,
one by one, to see the boy who
left thirty years before. The first one
tells how in the rain today her car
was hit, tells it time and time again
to all who come and once they find
she's not been hurt, they always ask,
first thing, *who hit your car?* She knows,
they know, the man. The boy leaves next day,
heading east, thinking when he's home
he must find out who moved in
last year to the house across the street
that had been vacant for six months.

Ordnance Plant

Two miles east the road comes to a T.
Straight ahead a chain-link fence
ten-foot high, barbed wire at the top.

It keeps them from the ordnance plant,
a place where they built the bombs
dropped in World War II.

In war the church boys chose the path
of peace and love. And yet that plant
spewed out weapons every day

and wheat the farmers grew and cream they sold
fed the makers of the bombs,
a topic that the preachers never talked about.

Instead they harped about the sins
of wearing wedding bands
and women chopping off their hair.

The Hastings Museum

If at a cocktail party
in the midst of erudite discussion
of the new exhibit at the Metropolitan
the opportunity arises he pontificates
about the newly discovered
Sunset at Montmajour
at the van Gogh in Amsterdam
that he saw on one of his frequent trips to Europe.

But at night he dreams
about the Museum of Natural History
in Hastings where Ralph, his Sunday school teacher,
took the Sunday school class twice a year.

The guide would point out the paintings
of the cowboys, six-shooters blazing,
but never show them the Catlin painting
of the squaw with the smiling baby in her lap,
at the far end of the hall, all alone.

Thoughts on Visiting the Barnes Museum in Philadelphia

In Lincoln two of these paintings
from just one wall of one room
of the Barnes would draw
the Sunday crowds to ooh and ah
who'd then drive home
and rave about the art to their friends
who stopped by after church
and then that night dream the dreams,
no more, no less,
than those back East who spent a week,
saw all the art in all the rooms.

Wood River Mennonite Church Inventory

Eight globes hanging down, casting
tepid light. Ten rows of benches on each side,
(women, children on the left, men on the right),
gum plastered on the undersides,
pried off and chewed again by antsy kids
kneeling for the half-hour prayers.
In the racks, fans from Appel's Funeral home,
stuck between the Life Songs and the Church hymnals.
The iron grate half-way up the middle aisle
where they huddle, bundled up, when it's twenty-five below.
The anteroom in back where baptized folk meet
Bishop Eicher, one-on-one, each spring and fall, to say
if they are right with God and fellowmen.
The table center-front on which deacon Art lays
the broken bread, the common cup.
The pulpit on the platform two steps up
from which the preacher thunders out the Word,
then prays on and on, as the boy
shifting side to side, peeks out,
still chewing on his gum,
to see who else is peeking out.

He knows he will be
something else

Volunteer Corn
(Wherever Seeds Will Fall)

More likely to mature if they were with their own
in the field a fence away, but here, amongst the wheat,
despite standing out two feet, and making twelve-inch ears,
the man who owns this field will hoe them out,
these stalks of corn, even if he tramples down the grain
to get to where they rise.

Ears missed by the picker
on its rounds last fall,
survived the January cold,
sprouted in the heat of May.
No fault of theirs or anyone's
the field was turned to wheat this year.

Baptism

Bishop Eicher drives
down from Milford that Sunday
like he does twice a year
to pass the cup, break the bread,
duties only he can do.
He and Sister Eicher
eat with the boy and his parents
to mark the solemn vows
the boy has made.
No other guests for once.

It troubles him, now out fifty years,
how he can recall
that first kiss, graduation gowns,
the wedding cake, babies' first cries,
but not the saying
of *I do, I will*, the pouring
of the water, the water
dripping down,
his rising up.

Photographs

The boy is five, Hope sixteen,
in that formal photograph.
Dad for once is Dad,
an unforced smile,
like the one that lit his sober face
when he saw Mom,
first time, at thirty-six.

Other times his mother
stands behind the lens.
Dad tries but cannot smile.
Photographs graven images
to his God, he says.

It's not until his father dies
the boy buys a camera,
to catch on film the huge Nebraska sky.
The neighbors beg him
to photograph their weddings
and anniversaries. In his darkroom
late at night he cannot wait
to see the faces in the negatives emerge
from the swirling chemicals.
Images of God.

Hardening of the Arteries

One evening while eating his mother's fried potatoes
and canned beef and lettuce and mayonnaise salad
after the boy tells his parents
about the new girl in second grade
and that he missed only one word on the spelling test,
the boy's father says that Otto Schultz has died—
hardening of the arteries, they think.

It takes him two hours to fall asleep.
His folks can't help much
when he runs downstairs twice
to ask what arteries are
and does *hard* mean *like cement.*

Before, he'd hoped to be a fireman
and then an electrician
who climbed poles in blizzards
when people lost power for three days.
For a spell, he dreamed of being
an architect. When he wakes
the next morning, he knows
he will be something else.

Jungle Doctor

His mom couldn't have discovered
"Jungle Doctor" in the *Gospel Herald*
(no book reviews then, and even though
he was a missionary he wasn't Mennonite)
nor would the doctor have made
the *Grand Island Independent.*
So the boy wonders where
she found Dr. White, whose books
told how he fought Schistosomiasis, cut
out cancers, and on Sundays preached the Word
in Tanganyika, books the boy devoured
like Mom's bread hot out of the oven.

He still keeps the first volume, safe between
Grey's Anatomy and Feigenbaum's *Principles
of Echocardiography* on the top shelf in his study.

Shaking Rugs

Saturday mornings
he does as he is told: picks up the rugs,
soiled from tracked-in filth
from barn and chicken coup,
drags them down five steps
to the concrete slab
outside the back door,
grasps each one, shakes it
violently. When the wind blows
from the east the dirt flies
into his face, stings his eyes.

He lugs them in and lays them down,
sure they are clean but one day
in twenty years when a professor screams
at him on rounds, says *you killed*
that patient, you
should have known,
and when the guilty one looks
the other way, will not admit
it was him, he realizes
some dirt will always stick.

The Sale Barn

Before looking in the clinic chart
at the weight of a patient
he tries to guess. He's always
within five pounds. He once told a nurse
and she asked him how he got to be so good
so he told her how he and his dad
would go on Saturdays to the cattle auction
in Grand Island, both wearing their striped overalls
with their wallets in the front pockets over their chests.
Dad would buy them each a wiener on a bun.
They'd sit third row up, engulfed in smoke
and smells of sweat and dung, watching
horseback men herd in the cattle,
then chase them out when they were sold.
The weights would flash up on a screen
and by the time he was ten his guess
was just as good as his dad's,
who was never off by much.

Here's to Herman and Charles

When he retires and they ask him
who were his mentors
and who influenced him the most,
he will think of Dr. Abboud,
physician, scientist, diagnostician,
mind so sharp
if you'd majored in basket weaving
for five years
within ten minutes
he'd be asking you questions
that showed he already
grasped the subject
as you never will
even after ten more years of study.
But then he will think of Herman,
only eight years of school,
who they say wired his house
himself when electricity came
and who hot-wired a Caterpillar,
and then cleared away
the barn and chicken shed
leveled by the tornado.
First time on such a machine.

And he will think about Dr. Hook,
head of medicine,
Distinguished Professor,
who taught him how
to treat patients
with infected heart valves
and who could
on July 1 of each year,
when the new interns came,
introduce all hundred people in the room
by first and surname by memory.
But then he thinks of Charles,
with not even a high school diploma,
but donor of five gallons of blood
so far and farmer who milks
all seventy-five cows before six a.m.,
plows the west forty by noon,
jury-rigs the broken grain grinder
so he can shell the corn
to feed the steers,
milks the cows again
and then goes to the school
that night to help
three other men
tear out the coal stove.

Watkins Salve

The boy didn't know if Watkins
was a doctor or a quack
but his dad thought Watkin's salve
would do for sore flesh
what the twice-a-year grape juice
did for the soul.

He'd smear it on the gash from a barbed-wire fence
on a calf's belly or on a cut on the boy's toe
from a rusty can. In two days
the calf would be eating oats again
and the boy racing barefoot to the barn and back.

The boy, now a man, remembers the patient
whose whole right leg was hot and red
from the germs deep in a bite
she thought would heal.
Too late he pumped in
Gentamycin and Carbenicillin,
the biggest guns he had.

What he needed was something
that would *draw out the badness*,
as his father would say.
He had no Watkins Salve.

Rounds and Chores

During those dire intern days
he'd rouse at 5 a.m.
after a blessed two hours
of sleep to see his eighteen patients,
    hoping that the morphine
had held for the man with the cold foot
from the blood clot, too sick
for the knife,
    hoping he would find a vein,
maybe in the foot, from which to take
the blood of the old lady with the gall
bladder and that he could find
it in fifteen minutes,
    hoping the garrulous man
in 413 would answer *yes* or *no*
when asked *do you have pain*,
not rant on about the food
that came too late,
    hoping he would have seen
the last patient in time to grab
scrambled eggs and toast before
the doctor at the top came
at 7 to round, fresh
from a normal night of sleep,
alert to interrogate young docs,
    hoping he would not mix up
the meds and vital signs of any two
housed in one room, that he would recall,
when he was quizzed, the fifteen

other things than heart attacks
that cause the chest to hurt
    remembering the morning chores
on January days when it was twelve below,
      thinking
this is not so bad.

How We Die

Some hold out for years, aneurysms
bulging out. They jog, they dance,
shoot 85s. Then die from the flu.

Others with hearts strong as iron pistons
have a flake break loose and block an artery,
are gone before the EMTs arrive.

Some, after heart attacks, refuse
to take the pills that slow the beat,
sneak chips and smokes when Martha's
gone to bed, still drink with the boys
on Monday nights, and slip away in 15 weeks.

His friend Ken drove tractors all his life,
a careful man who had a wife and little girl.
Knew how to steer, but passing
through the 6-foot ditch between the road
and field, the Farmall tipped
and rolled, crushed him
underneath a wheel.

And Otto lost an arm pulling out
stalks of corn from the picker
(should have turned the engine off).
His life bled out.

Worst of all was Red.
After six shots, five beers one night,
he weaved back and forth
walking down the road,
dressed in black. Dead
on the spot. The driver
was his son.

The Plowing Poet

No iambs or anapests,
no dachtyls on a John Deere,
only putt-putt spondees.

Cacophony of sounds: no assonance
or consonance the squalking of the birds
jumping in the dirt to grab for worms.

No rhyme or rhythm: free verse
the frantic rushing of the mice
escaping from the tractor tire.

Songs sung out above the roar
to a girl he thinks about.
Apostrophe?

Conceit: the red-winged blackbirds
nuns with banners
marching down a center aisle.

He yanks the rope to raise
the plow before he turns around,
yanks it once again to set it down. No
enjambment.

Quenching the Spirit

When he is twelve
the fear wakes him
at night just before
the banty rooster crows

and it is why at 66
he walks out in the middle
of the preaching of the Word
to write the poem.

Rings of years

Shingling the Barn Roof

Why his father let him climb
he'll never know—a boy of twelve,
eaves up eighteen feet,
the roof's peak eighteen more.
He hammers in the cedar shakes,
no safety belt, no net below,
thrilling to a task
he thought only grownups could do,
never once looking down.

And now in later years,
high on the academic roof,
he finds himself gazing down
to where he's been,
wondering how he'd reached this height,
wondering when the shingling
is done, are there other barns?

Silos and TV Towers

They head a hundred miles east
to cousin Albert's dairy farm.
The boy wakes before the cows, scales
the silo, crawls inside, wades through
chopped up stalks, pretends he's swimming
through the ocean that he's never seen.
Coming home, he pleads with Dad
to drive them by the quarter-mile high
steel tower sending TV waves
across Nebraska skies. He dreams
of climbing to the top, swaying
in the prairie wind, gazing east
as far as Iowa, having ascended
so far up he loses sight of Dad and Mom.

Back home, no silos, only a barn with a haymow.
Just a radio so Dad can hear
the Mennonite Hour on Sunday
and the price of corn every other day of the week.

Seagulls in Nebraska

No one he asks knows much
about the white birds with gray wings
that follow him on the B John Deere,
swooping down to grab worms
turned up by the two-bottom plow.
So he looks them up
in the *World Book Encyclopedia* and all
his people say is really? when he tells them
they are seagulls that have flown
1,500 miles west to get here.
And they laugh when the boy says
those birds are crazy, stopping over
this 40 acre patch of dirt.

After Dad moves them to Virginia,
the boy never gets around to writing
to old neighbors about the gulls that snatch clams
from the water, soar high, drop them on rocks
and then gulp the sweet meat.

Cottonwood Coffin

I want, when I am gone,
for them to find a cottonwood
from the old home place,
chop it down,
use the wood
to make my final box.

I hope the stump
will show the rings
of years of growth,
each ring outside
for one whole year
for all to see,
no rot at the core
that would in time
have killed the tree.

Acknowledgments and Credits

Grateful acknowledgment is given to editors and others involved in prior publication of the poems below, sometimes in a slightly different version:

"District 37," *CMW Journal.*

"Ordnance Plant," *CMW Journal.*

"Wood River Mennonite Church," *CMW Journal.*

"Hardening of the arteries," *Art House America.*

"Blessed be the tie that binds," *Art House America.*

"My father's spade," *Art House America.*

"Passing out tracts in Grand Island," *Art House America.*

"Grandmother Gascho," *Lincoln Underground.*

"Rural Route 3," *Lincoln Underground.*

"van Gogh in Nebraska," *Lincoln Underground.*

The Author

Joseph Gascho was born in Grand Island, Nebraska. His father was a farmer and the pastor of the small church (Wood River Mennonite) Joseph attended. He went to a one-room country school until he moved, at age thirteen, with his parents to Harrisonburg, Virginia, to attend Eastern Mennonite High School. He graduated from Eastern Mennonite College and received his medical degree from the University of Virginia.

Since finishing his training in cardiology, Gascho has been on the faculty of first the University of Virginia School of Medicine and then Penn State Hershey College of Medicine, where he is presently Professor of Humanities and Medicine.

Many of his poems are related to medicine, and he has had numerous poems published in medical journals. He is also a photographer, and much of his photography focuses on medicine. He has had numerous one-person photography exhibits and has several permanent exhibits of his photography at Penn State Hershey. He was awarded first prizes for both his poetry and his photography in *Annals of Internal Medicine*.

Gascho is married to Barbara Brunk, the Virginia girl with whom the Nebraska boy fell in love, a nurse-chaplain in an ALS clinic. He has two children, a son who is a professional harpsichordist and a daughter who is a pastor. Gascho, who lives in Hummelstown, Pennsylvania, is a member of Community Mennonite Church, Lancaster.

CPSIA information can be obtained
at www.ICGtesting.com
Printed in the USA
BVHW01s2316010318
509525BV00001B/12/P